Blasphemer's Wheel

Blasphemer's Wheel

Selected and New Poems

by Patrick Friesen

For Collette,
it's been great
working with you
this year,
Best
Patrick Friesen
april 24/95

Turnstone Press

Turnstone Press
607-100 Arthur Street
Winnipeg, Manitoba
Canada   R3B 1H3

Turnstone Press gratefully acknowledges the assistance of
the Canada Council and the Manitoba Arts Council.

Some of the new poems appeared in *Border Crossings,*
Poetry Canada Review and *Prairie Fire.*

Cover art: Eva Fritsch

Text design: Manuela Dias

This book was printed and bound in Canada by
Kromar Printing for Turnstone Press.

Canadian Cataloguing in Publication Data

Friesen, Patrick, 1946-

Blasphemer's wheel

ISBN 0-88801-179-2

I. Title.

PS8561.R496B4 1994   C811'.54   C94-920050-6
PR9199.3.F749B4 1994

By the same author:

You Don't Get to Be a Saint (Turnstone, 1992);

Flicker and Hawk (Turnstone, 1987);

The Shunning (Turnstone, 1980);

Contents

from
the lands i am

waiting for the gods

at night dripping mares stand on the beach
white and honey manes
                              not a muscle in motion
                              they look out to sea
a step
and ghostly splash

in the morning water swims over the moon-prints
this must be the place where I wait for nothing

some kind of memory

blood is not thickest
when we kiss deeply
but it swells full
when the veins carry
the echo of father footsteps
and winter horses
startled at their drinking

teutonia

riding the sea for two weeks
toward the delivered land,
engines grinding below,
they were closer to home than they knew.

their portion
as thin as the youngest son,
their purpose
accordingly brisk,
they adhered through the night
the water gave them.

(pray for guidance
and for grace)

not a man
knew the sea well enough
to call himself sailor;
they stood strange and stiff
before the wind.
not a man
knew the sea,
yet they remained;
unwilling citizens
in the slope and shift
of the waves.

in the morning the smoke of a fog
led through Atlantic deluge;
each night the sun went down to the sea.
and always, higher, coiling birds,
white and fire-winged, shrilled.

stony land

lean and stark apart,
striding across the stubbled earth,
the old man knew the hairs of sorrow.
each knuckle of his hands a fist,
each finger a bent direction.

(he knew the plod of a slow horse
with dust like chaff at its feet,
the Sunday chat of hens
making a stillness in the barn.)

and he knew the clatter of clay
on a box, where his woman lay.

his mouth a wound,
his voice harsh
and his words graceless,
he sat gaunt in his straight chair,
unlamenting.

almost nothing stops

we cannot wear weeds
forever
    the wind
parts them
    the earth
steams, it undulates
and meets the slanting rain
our lovers lie with us
    the columbine
astounds us
beside the road
red-winged blackbirds
sing from cattails,
illogical,
    our friends
embrace us
    our brothers and sisters
remind us
we are not alone
our brothers and sisters
remind us that
we are alone

we dress for the seasons
and find you
where the poplar floats its seeds
where wind
drives the rain relentlessly

Marijke: my first-born

in the face of the sun
scatter the petals of the warm, pale rose;
the hours diminish, for the moon
will be split in silver.

soon comes the rush
of returning rain; the young one,
in a basket of water,
issues cramped through the loins.
she dances the old canal;
she takes the time
to move without a sound.

I wonder at her fiery heart and the ocean;
I wonder at the furrow and her name.

hard chair

sitting on a hard chair
between the conversation
    and her dreams
her palsy is stilled
as she gathers herself for death

each child tore
the sinews of her wrists
    each child meant
        the intrusion
of the stars
    each child
the fear of reeling
        drunken
   space

    only when the blood issue
ceased   and the turning
      of leaves dried
   did her hands feel
the tremble of their ruin

      her hands move now
    to stillness
and lie like pools of water
   in her lap

from
bluebottle

bluebottle

he died on a stone pillow
his hand on a bannister
there was nothing between us

    for the moment

I was the staircase and the last touch
he the debut
between touch and ghost

I heard a bluebottle in the blind

    the droning was   summer days
    chewing the stems of lilac leaves

    the fall of yellow afternoons

    suns glinting
    on the blue hood of our '53 dodge
    and father hoisting me
    to the hot fender for a photograph

    sitting still
    and father brushing sandflies off my back

between touch and ghost
while I heard time
everything happened at once

accomplice

I was at the funeral

all the brethren
my stiff-necked mennonites
carried the coffin
and sang

their amazing grace
made me weep for old days

father died
wanting to die
I consented
and felt his blessing

I was there

I smelled heat
off the pavement
saw it shimmer
above the field

I was there
his accomplice
among idle worshippers
who would not let go

I heard the buzzing of a bottled fly

bread was flesh of the dead
I could not eat

later
in the basement
of the house he built
I whispered my rites

closet

I finger the khaki shirt
he wore on his last working day
before he unbuttoned

along the collar   stain of sweat
faint salt smell of him alive
even as he lies
past mattering in the grave

work pants sharply creased
have fallen from the wooden hanger
I see wrinkles behind the knees
where he stooped or bent

lenses of the eye-glasses
reveal striations
of his eye-lashes on dust

I can imagine what he saw
as he lay thin and bare
in that dark place

crows

almost violet crows with bright eyes
straddle furry mounds on the highway shoulder

they pick at winter's yellow entrails
their narrow gaze strips the flesh away

when a semi blows them off the road
they flap over straw stubble in a straggly flock

their cawing in open fields

without ghost

I am without ghost
simply shivering
as her wet mouth makes me
flesh again

stripped
I am without wings
real and rooted
in the sun and rain

I have nothing to hold back

my ghost hovers near the ceiling
dispassionately observes
    a raven beaking the sprawl
    feather and bone

    strokes of light
    dazzle in the drizzling rain

    the highway is timeless
    by the broken feast on its shoulder
    flight is suspended
    in the perfect pinning of flesh
    on flesh

breasts

it is only the fourth month

in an alchemy that astounds me
her breasts soften   feel liquid to my touch

long ago   before man
unearthed blood in words
this silkiness must have brushed him
told him   woman held the moon

the skin is milky
nipples like leather
brown as earth

I hold the plump underneath of one breast
in the curve of my palm
there is in its swaying an easy fullness
there is a generosity I had not known

summer going on fall

a heap of cement blocks
and a garden beside them

my barefoot daughter
eats apples off the ground
and sings an old story

the willow leaves are sticky
from last night's fogging
weeping birch too
and strawberries
and the oak out front

I swat at a fugitive mosquito
honing in suicidal as any zero combat plane

the sun is a hammer
driving my head down on my neck
until my eyes glaze over with the ache
and I sit in a buzzing tunnel
not moving

from somewhere my wife's voice says
no strawberries today
the bees must have fallen in the fog
no strawberries rest of the summer

and I say the effect couldn't be that fast

but then why no strawberries

my little girl's singing
about when she used to be a little girl
(she's only three
which seems young enough to me)

my wife points out the pruning she's done on the dogwood
and I notice through my haze
how japanese the dogwood looks
the intricacy of angles or something
maybe a thwarted kind of economy
whatever

the buzzing continues
and a cement truck rumbles by
with its space capsule turning
the foundations of another house within it

an acorn plummets
bouncing off the sidewalk into my lap
I crack it open
my wife says it's poison
I chew it anyway
birds eat them   why not me

and still my daughter singing

    I useta be happy
    I useta be mad
    I useta be happy
    so . . . that's what I had

and as if a carnegie hall of men
thrilled to every note and word
and she afloat on their applause

    thank-you gentlemens

and the sun's got me
the world's reeling
and it's christmas in my head

god rest her
god rest her   merry

Marijke's poem

when she dances
            the wolf turns to grass
when she sings
            he turns to air

she can walk on him
she can breathe him

when I sing I breathe ash
when I dance I trip on creepers

taking care
I walk shod
take shallow breaths

I fear the wolf and the encounter

give me tongue to exult
give my feet quickness

I sing the moment
between tooth and bone
I dance at the diggings
while my flesh goes down

from
The Shunning

he had disobeyed. had waded barefoot in the creek before the
weather was warm enough. you could easy have got a cold she
said. she brought out a spool of #10 thread and tied his ankle to
a tree with a 5 foot length.

break that and you get strapping.

mother hoeing

her red arms
her eight-month belly
her hair tied into a knot

then the bright hoe raised high
slashing down like a sun
again   again
and mother stoops to pick up the mangled snake
slings it over the fence   a yellow rope

she wipes her hands on her apron
nostrils wrinkling she turns to me   smell this
I inhale the musk and grease of her hands

his mother thought it was the second coming   one taken   one left. her eye has wandered for a moment. when she turned back she alone stood in mid-garden   hoe in hand.

for that instant she stood bewildered. christ had returned and left her behind. that was not her horror   the taken son was. to lose her only child   the flesh she loved more than herself   the flesh that would be made word.

her eyes looked for directions in the garden   in the sky. there were no flames or winds. everything was still   as before   yet all lost in a moment.

then she saw corn stalks wave at garden's end. she ran to hug the boy with corn silk for his beard. a prodigal son   a kind of ghost   baffled by her love.

black horses
muzzles glittering with frost
chains like frozen chimes

black horses
dragging logs into the firelight
their shadows rear across trees

and I'm wide-eyed all night

voices shouting commands
echoing from farther forests
and no one in sight

and this is how I dream of emptiness

rooster crows the sun
and I know what must be done
before it crows again

I dress quickly
walk out   boots in hand

running for the henhouse
I smell the heap of smashed eggs
grab the startled rooster and twist his neck
throw him on the stinking eggs

hens flutter as I flounder   reaching
tearing with my hands   my teeth
spitting blood and feathers
fat headless hens dancing on broken shells
the room all dust and feathers
and my voice shaking rafters
my words sailing through walls
no   I bellow   no   no

and then it is still   so still

sun slants in at the windows
on the spattered floor   on my untied boots

from Johann's farm a cock crows
the sun will not be denied

this man   less than a man
stands these days in doorways
this man   my man   I
flinch at this distance I have run

where fields grow bones
and nothing breathes
a graveyard I have circled before
now stumble   stand in the middle
turning   squint at the apparent edge   the trees

this distance will not be forgiven

I must come back
sit on benches
if I am to be loved again

but how do I come back?

forgive them   he whispers
limp hair and sweating
forgive them   he says
then his eyes open   ask why

of the world
mother weeps for him

his brother shivers at noon

a choir of soldiers sings   shoulder to shoulder

he smells rope at his wrists
the approaching rain

raises his head in the dark
forgive   he says
at last
me

a silver fall   water
fall arcing   aching
cock crow

singing the hollow

hallow
the hollow   singing

still
in that cold face
singing yes   yes   yes
singing   still
at cock crow
at caught cock crow
in the face of

no god
know

black wings flapping

in one appalling twitch
here   beside this creek

blood spilling   worthless
blood seeping in earth   and heaven this night

where tomorrow

red sky

at morning
sailor's warning

the crouped child choking
and mother holding him over a steaming kettle

the child sprawled on gravel   licking his blood

the child   rolling his pantlegs to the knees
wading down twin creek   cattails bowing
this boy   his feet and calves mud-smeared
is man here   the caught corpse

one hand in water
one boot off   the other untied
his white foot nudging the rifle stock

his temple   a blue hole the bullet made

✧

Or this.

a woman walking home from church
her shawl loosens and slips to her shoulders
she pauses   removes combs and pins
lifts her face to the sky and shakes out her fiery hair

behind her the sun and golden withers
of a horse reaching for grass
beneath the bottom strand of barbed wire

a horse   the sun
and almost everyone shielding their eyes

on a sunday

thursday afternoon thunder
I come in from seeding
hoping to work other fields

and my Carolina's willing

I scrub at the basin
comb back my wet hair

cool air rustles at the window
we undress and stand
shivering   staring at flesh

the deep rift of her spine curving to buttocks
her fingers like feathers raising hairs on my arms
my flat stomach   her soft-bellied urge

Carolina takes my hand
and draws me beneath the quilt

I smell rain at the window

How she bunches freshly-cut gladioli in one quick hand and
thrusts them into a pitcher. Her familiar fingers spreading the long
stalks   fluffing petals open.

How she walks   straight as a hollyhock   a milk-pail in each
hand.

How she curves her head forward and to one side to watch the
young one suck.

How like a girl she looks even though she is young.

the ground he chose   to kneel
where he kneeled in mud
where he began to untie his boots
shivering   his hands shaking
and the sun settling in the grass

I know him   not well enough
I know his overalls were wet from knees to cuffs
his eyes were blue
I know he carried a poplar branch to goad the trigger

soft eyes   I think
soft eyes and blue as if the sky bled them

what he smelled at last
water rotting in the reeds
or air sweet with clover

what he saw at dusk
light walking away across fields
the hole a sky can be
what he saw   water rippling in a ring

brummer barking in the trees somewhere

the man johann
who fished here with a crooked nail   he said
who splashed in this creek with his woman
when the sun was high and work could wait
johann   who told how they ducked each other
how they swam underwater and exploded through the surface
     near drinking cows
the cattle lurching   front legs in water
backing up the bank   their large heads swaying

the flames he endured   the iron in him

johann   I remember   leaning against a fence
his bony hands gesturing as he spoke

around us the wreckage of his farm
a rusting harrow   bone buildings careening
grass surging against the barn

johann remembered his brother
who tore the curtain and went blind
who taught johann fear   and not fear
that the child dies no matter what
and a man carries his funeral with him
you never know how many people you bury with a man
nor how many are born again

come   said johann   let's go back to the house
ruth bakes bread today
it's good when it's still warm and the butter melts

listen   he whispered

that rasping sound   that's a yellowhead
see it   over there   near the creek

and I saw
a blackbird with a sun for its head

O dass ich tausend Zungen hätte

from
Unearthly Horses

pa poem 1: firstborn

pa dropped the baby
when he heard it speak
scared as hell to hear the young one talk
thinking of the devil
and the tongue that can take you anywhere

pa confessed the road ahead
his and the boy's
smelled the day of his death   and the child
barely out of diapers
pa glimpsed the future I was going to say
but what he really saw was
the kid on his rear where he fell
with his eyes pinched tight   mouth wide open
and the shadow of the word
that named him dad

pa heard the first word
like headwaters of a flood
tumbling and dark ahead
and pa with his eyes wide
stared at the boy   bare as the day of his birth
and howling with abandon

pa dropped his firstborn
and sat there in the kitchen
alone   and remembering . . .
. . . there was nothing
there

but his sheltered heart
and the saying   da da

pa poem 2: toward eternity

I didn't know he was that alone
except maybe for ma he was by himself
and when you see the man swelling with cancer
in some stiff bed   his brain saying it can't take anymore
but something in him strong enough to bear all
his eyes following ma when she leaves the room
or when she sits beside his bed   her eyes numb
his hand reaching for her breasts
25 years of affirmation in that gesture
as if he was making memory
and the man so perfectly alone with fear
looking up   seeing blindly across the room
his son   blasted with world and God
the child who startled him with utter betrayal

how the whole man can ache to be remembered mercifully
and this is how he learns to say goodbye
plucking bare words from the language of pain

and finally   for me   the man no longer clutching his robe
                                        about him
floating away   as if he had never been
so light and thin   as if he had never swung a hammer

when you see a man vanishing before you
your father   the pain in his eyes
clears and there is no love nor sorrow   the eyes break
looking   as ma said   toward eternity
then you know the question and admiration
are all you have

pa poem 3: standing the night through

like jesus' death
pa's death split everything into before and after
and nothing was healed

before he died I stalled pa's '67 ford in the churchyard
in july in still heat with mirages on the highway

after   I drove into the city to get my funeral clothes
and I'd be lying if I didn't say I saw a falling star
near ste. anne right in front of me in the middle of the windshield

one thing I remember well from the spring before he left
that was the night I woke and lit a candle in the porch
thinking of pa walking off his pain in a bedroom 40 miles away
a locomotive whistled in the switching yard and a breeze doused
                                        the flame
the kind of thing you read about   the cliché come alive

after   I stood the night through in pa's basement
writing his obituary as if it was mine
handed it to the minister
watched him stroke out 'died' and scribble in 'passed away'
as if there was no end to it
even for me

pa poem 4: naked and nailed

I remember those carpenter's hands
thick fingers drumming the table
fingers that tightened around my biceps
lifted me right off the kitchen floor
down basement steps
and there we were in front of the furnace
me pleading across your knee   both of us wishing we were
                                         someplace else
but you not spoiling the child
and you swung that leather high
me twisting to look up   your arm flung out
seeing you naked and nailed like a child to a tree

how could there be so much love?

I wish I could have seen you sidestep
or shout the words of your hurt
even better I would have loved to see you leaping
on your long narrow feet   howling
and sweat flying from that fine muscled chest

what's a father if he doesn't let out
the whirling dervish the gypsy or the juggler?

you one-eyed monster
you saw more than you let on
maybe more than you ever knew
but you couldn't find the words for me

you rowing that boat into mother's dreams
someplace out there   maybe still looking for the words
and one night with me sleeping creepy
you'll find them and you'll find me

sitting in bed shivering
maybe before I find you
you'll tap me on the shoulder
I'll turn
I'll recognize you

and see   you old dead man
how I start with my grievance
and always end up with this Goddamned love
but I tell you that won't happen everytime
or it'll kill me

pa poem 5: singing elijah

I wanted to tell you what I'm doing
at least be ready when you come around at night
I tried to remember what I was thinking or doing when you left
and you know   not much really changed
what was true in 1971 is still true
nothing happens day to day does it?   nothing new

yet some things need saying
we both knew I almost said the final thing
you wanted to stop your ears
but I never did say it   not to you
it would have hurt you then
you would have thought the last days were upon us
but now I'm saying it
because you came to me and maybe it's what you want

jerusalem is dead   stone dead sea dead
something old men dream
as they gaze into empty days

there's nothing new here
people have lived this desolation for years
there are not many of your kind   a handful
who still believe as if 2000 years hadn't occurred
that's how it's supposed to work   isn't it?
the crucifixion then   and today   nothing between

you were a mystery man pa
lost in some kind of miracle
but you received the law
like everyone else   you were found
and you thought your children must be found
uprooted into light

I can't speak for the others
almost don't have the heart to speak for myself
think of me as lost   living
with one foot in the shade
trying to be true and double-crossing you every step of the way
it's something to live with

these days I'm poking around again
found the old grounds   and the grave
pa   I sang 'beulah land' the other day
'sweet sweet beulah land'

just thought I'd let you know
I'm starting to sing   no one's really heard me yet
and I'm not singing jerusalem
I'm singing 'beulah land'   I'm singing elijah
because I see ahead where I shed my clothes
maybe hang them in a closet
and disappear

pa poem 6: among the glads

when the pain got bad pa's nerves went
couldn't endure squabbles at the table
he'd leave pale and sweating for the garden
where he'd kneel among the glads and go through his ritual
whatever it was he did   touching or stroking stems
something to soothe him I guess   assure himself he was really there

and sometimes he'd strike out with an uncoiling rage
hit my brother once with his belt   gouged flesh with the buckle
an accident pure and simple   he never thought of the metal
but it was a rage that made ma speak out
it must have scared her to make her turn on pa like that
in front of the kids telling him he was wrong

what pa said or did after that I don't know
but I think the man must have holed up
probably in the basement   standing near the furnace
wondering what it was he was doing
how he could flail one of his boys like that

and I'd be surprised if he wasn't remembering his dad
and whatever lay between them
the boy aching   alone   between steinbach and la broquerie
his mother something shadowy beneath blankets
slipping toward her death that night
words rasping in his father's throat
harrowing his life away in stone fields

grandpa and pa   I could confuse those men if I thought too much
                                          about them
and how he could thrash me   as if I was someone else
he usually had control of himself
thrashed me in the basement for something I did
pa   my dad   teaching me across his knee
ma said it hurt him more than me   it must have

44

pa poem 7: rehearsing for sunday

pa sang real well
I used to hear him at home   rehearsing for sunday
sometimes just him and ma   sometimes with other people

ma played piano   the others standing behind her
pa maybe sucking a couple of sen sens
and sometimes I'd be lying in bed almost asleep
and I'd hear ma's voice like glass   or maybe water on glass
I'd forget the bad notes
and I'd listen past the melody and the harmony
right through to pa's voice
almost clear not quite   like a cello with smoke at the edge
filling the spaces just when you realized they were there

that's it   everyone else was singing to make those intervals
and pa letting them hang a bit   just enough to make you want to
                                                         close them
then swooping in there as if that's the only thing could happen right then

pa sang real well
until his lungs went and then   the last days   his throat

one sunday he and I sat facing each other in the living room
his voice was hoarse   I hoped he would clear it
but he didn't   or couldn't   and that harsh voice grew into stories
of his father   and I thought he was forgiving him for something
though the dates were all wrong   I wanted to hallow this dying
but I had not learned to sing

pa poem 8: on the beach

my feet dangling from the dock I watched
pa   hands at his sides   alone on the beach   staring at ma
up to her knees in west hawk lake
leaning forward to splash cold water on her thighs
ma's hair tied at the back
and her laughing that clear laugh with germaine clinging to her
     legs

september leaves were turning
ma's laugh echoed forever across the empty lake
as if we were the only ones alive

I was shivering and stood to leave
pa looked over at me
I was 10 and saw what was happening
though it didn't occur to me till now
that pa was riveted by knowing
there was nothing more
on earth for him

the man who invented himself

1.
I remind you of the man who invented himself
out of clay and spit   amino acids if you will
out of photographs and dreams
out of the right hand of god and baptism   he invented himself

he thought as a young man he would read palms in the pub
or display his memory for the names of spanish poets
he writhed in fevers of justice   saw they weren't just
and was almost lost in a map of emotions

the man who invented himself
failed to explain it all to himself
no matter where he left a distinct impression
he walked toward obscurity

2.
after splashing for a while. my son sits quietly in the bath
examining his fingers   how they wrinkle
his feet   his penis   and whatever else he can reach

3.
in 1977 I sat in the northern square of the golden cathedral
when lawrence came to guadalajara he saw this cathedral first
from a distance   hills between   this dome glowing in the west
I remembered reading that in one of his travel books
I walked back to my hotel   a shadow on mexican stones

4.
'I once was lost/but now am found'

the man who invented himself didn't write that
but he heard it the day he was born and couldn't forget it
you might say that line was the true mystery for him

it gave him something to do
you could hear him humming between drinks
or laughing or mocking or posturing
and more than once he turned the line around

the man who invented himself invented mirrors
though he was told it had been done before
you can imagine how upsetting that was
to be such a fool caught with his foot in the door
but he knew his history and everyone was wrong
he knew it hadn't been done before

5.
I thought just now   how to continue
the life and times of this devious man
how to keep your interest in one I hardly know myself
a man not particularly interesting
who likes to believe he invented himself
and longs   like all his kind   for the grave

my son interrupts me
calling to share yet another anatomical discovery
you and me dad   he confides   it's kind of touching
the only real solidarity I've ever felt

as I leave the bathroom I turn to the mirror
and   for an instant   see myself turn toward myself

6.
you're always where you've been
said the man who invented himself
you're always where you're going
(I remember him as a child)

7.
'there's going to be a meeting /
in the air'   he sang   he liked the tune
imagining the invention of selves
remembering the streets of towns and cities
the songs   *amazing grace* on home street
or *green river* in guadalajara   from a shortwave radio

songs that reminded him of other songs
sidewalks that recalled other sidewalks and other towns
in the evening a bath   then out drinking with the others
and always singing   in his heart   'I once was found'

easter

it's time

children   this is where easter happened
on this street   at this tree
this poplar   well I climbed it
and saw grandfather's pine miles away
and here   on this lawn
one summer evening I heard the *moonlight sonata*

I begin to shiver
there's always this danger of losing control
when I go back
when everything true stands before me
and there's no way of letting my children know
I just point out the objects

and maybe one day   if I'm lucky
one of them remembers the tree
the way a breeze rustled leaves that day
how the old man stared at something not there

oh christ   doesn't matter

father didn't show me where he stood
some days I make the rounds
remembering where I think I saw him
photos where he and the place are the same
I try to stand on his ground
wondering where the man was

I tear at boards
pull nails with my teeth
dismantle the house with all my might
toppling history on home street
to father digging the cellar in 1945
singing toward his wedding

what could keep him here
this earthly love

or not worshipping her body   loving her
or the garden   revealing
what couldn't be shown   what he could never say

I can say though that easter is here
that mom whistled my dog to the post here
that pa tied the dog here
that they slaughtered him here

I can say
that my birthday   each summer   is here
in this field
that I see how the world turns here
dawn to dusk

and this is it
how the world happens for me
this is the place
I am here
wherever I am I am
here

shakespeare's horses

shakespeare's horses are galloping
from the woods you can hear bridle and harness
first you see them as shadows
then they spurt into a sunlit field
snorting as they're reined in
sweat sprays from their rearing heads
you can smell them   touch them   they are after all horses

they are not monarchists

and my neighbour's dog
the one that pisses against my apple tree
is not a communist

the apple tree itself
if it in fact had legs to run away with
could be considered a masochist
but it is not

and me   I've been planning for some time to take a holiday
a permanent one   give the kiss off to all
who think I should believe one way or another

gobshits who want to spread religion
democracy or socialism   or preach the approaching end

let me say it like this:

things from the head pass through mirrored rooms
become enamoured of themselves   like movie stars
they play themselves to perfection

the idea is to make real the idea   isn't it?

'surgeons do your work

life is unbearable
give us rights
give us power

knowing a child can kill
or be in the way
destroy children

doctor put her away
she is miserable and not doing anyone any good

open your text
show us the correct way

somehow   with your knife
make us happy   cut out the doldrums
the pain sorrow and regret

surgeon   give us choices'

the idea is to know
but to know what?

that the inquisition the purges the reformation
the cultural revolution the hearings
the progressives and traditionalists
the missionaries social workers and comrades
queens premiers and chairmen are all assassins?

to know all our remedies mire us deeper
that each new order sinks us more profoundly into what we are

that nothing can be done
because there are too many busy doing
the extravaganza carries on

that this rendering of time
may simply give way to another

comfort the dying   that is a calling
and as for the rest   a horselaugh

if you can find it in you
beside the sorrow

turning home

1.

    'turn
to your mother
whom you have torn
who has become something unknown
a wise son would comfort his mother

but you sadden her
she always thought you must have come from a better world
brooded that maybe she shouldn't have had children
when she read of evil
murders   pillage   rape
a child strung from a streetlamp
bayonets   flies
the abattoirs of civilization
the courts   riflemen   the great world religions

she has a sense of the quick
life death and pain   worrying for your death
a traffic mishap   aneurism
the sudden moment when there are no more choices

and the smell of alcohol on your breath'

mother   I used to turn to you
when I wasn't snarling downstairs
at the end of a rope

'a mother knows history   she sees her son
walking or crawling through it   where are you?
she told you stories
and through her sorrow she loves you'

I turned to you   I had to
turn from your fear
my teeth must have been sharp
it's true I tore you   however

tell me about the blueprint you received   you and father
one gave and the other took
one thrashed me while the other suffered
one fed me into the other's teeth
neither wanting to carry on like this
but doing it anyway   for my good
for paradise   for the slaughterhouse

2.
I was looking out the window
staring straight at eden   then
in a blink of my eyes it went
hard to forgive whoever/
whatever pulled the blinds

I was alone
you know how it is
when you're haunted
flinging words at ghosts
beneath the basement steps
and the ghost runs away
to a place you'll find later

I was alone   once
I was the wonder   mother's last joy
before I crossed the threshold
(growing up   good god
I climbed trees   swaying over rooftops
I saw the whole world

remember   in space
titov said he didn't see God
and we shivered at his audacity
shook out heads at his simplicity   but I too
didn't see God at the top of the maple
only the world   and me   and not much between)

grandfather's spooky farm   almost deserted at easter
only barney and prince in the barn and one cat at the saucer
I was sitting in an abandoned wagon
long grass poking through shrunken snow
pretending the chase was on and my life in the balance
mimicking grandfather with harsh shouts   snapping the lines
magnificent horses   all muscle and buttocks   pell mell for hell

like the western movies   ma
I've dropped the reins
I'm poised in a crouch
about to leap onto those lunatic horses

it's not that I don't want to jump
but I keep turning to you from a distance
trying to remember you
wanting to tell you my love for you
afraid the words will be used against me
somehow to perpetuate your martyrdom   my cruelty
wanting to say something simple and true before our end

can you believe that all these years
I felt the burden of your love?
that I am a child of god
with no way to tell you?

that I have earned everything through lies
longing always for childhood

die seligen stunden . . . o blick des lichts

mutter
noch immer die freude in deinem spiel
mit den chinesen   mit meinen kindern
deine schlauen blauen augen   die geschmeidigen beine
ein mädchen das nirgends gehört
ausser zum innern kind   die erinnerung bäume

noch von schatten reichen

wanting to kiss you   or wave
some gesture   an earthly intimation

gottes kind

asking forgiveness for my human treachery

3.
grandma is a mischievous girl raising her skirts
to wade the creek or maybe to show her legs to the gypsies
who knows what the girl in grandma thinks
pretends sometimes she can't hear
when something's said she doesn't want to know

her head bows over water   looking for fish
on either side niko and marijke bow too
their hair tangled touches grandma's

mutter
mit dir
bin ich ganz
ohne dich

she teaches them reflections
stirs water with her fingers
their faces bending/dancing

birds   she whispers   carry messages
trees point to god

with marijke she walks up the rise   arm in arm
marijke becoming
the leggy young woman grandma was
and still is   somewhere

it was here mother told me her dream
how father beckoned with his arm
sitting in a boat   mid-river
how she called   saying   wait for me
but first she had to tend the children
when she returned he was gone

this is a peaceful place she said
and sad   I thought
mother   I'm with you
trying to be whole again
though you know it's a trick   don't you?
watching you search for niko
hearing him shout   'you can't find me'

niko
curled around a branch
naked   almost
lost in the foliage
grandma pretending not to find him
poking bushes with a stick   muttering to herself
then finally looking up
sun in the leaves   shading her eyes
'you can't hide that easily'
she laughs
'I can see you
you little auca'

and he grins
wild-haired
doesn't move
doesn't believe her
because he can't see her

that's how the day goes
how every day has ever gone
turning like this   mischievously
whether the stars bark or bite

that's how the sun finds us today
among the stones and trees
spinning the day away   always turning home

4.
so a son   in his way   comforts his mother
learns to show his ambiguous love

and everywhere murder persists
for all the fabulous causes   for all the wealth
raskolnikov because there's nothing else
a mother leaping into the south saskatchewan with her babies

that's how the sun finds us everyday
among the stones and trees
spinning the day away   always turning home

from
Flicker and Hawk

nothing in the mirror

1.

something about all the rooms I have inhabited
the way they were cluttered cloisters
or how I sit cross-legged in this room today
eating oysters with my cat
reminds me of someone   or maybe a mirror

a woman lying on a narrow bed
moonlight slipping across the sill
touches the darkness of her eyes

she is asleep   unless
I look again
and begin to understand the wound
within her sleep

her endurance on that wind-swept terrain
where she stands alone in snow
remembering children at fox and goose

while others wonder at the memory
she wonders at its ruin
and then   because she has earned the strength she
     was given
she turns toward the light

she sleeps where she threw herself
skirt caught high on her thigh
dark hair across her throat

when she wakes she smiles
and rises   opening her blouse

2.

I heard a voice in the backyard
singing *das grab ist leer*

I went to the window
saw sheets and pillow cases flapping

the wind   in march
was cornflower blue

3.

something about the river
I heard ice grind in my sleep
something fierce and neccessary
tempted me

sun rising in april
I stood on the assiniboine
heard ice boom in the distance
and suddenly cracks scattering around my feet
I waited for water to open beneath me

vater sterbt

a man with one blind eye
who meant well

tod

kalt

there was something about rivers
perhaps that each one held a reflection
waiting for me

wasser

she walked there
sometimes I met her

once I found her yellow scarf

4.

I was waiting at new year's
for the woman who knew every dance

waiting for midnight
when lights went out
and everyone kissed

a woman gave me her tongue
who was she?

I hid in another room
a window stood open
when I spoke I saw the clouds of words
how they vanished when I held my breath
I wondered at my foolishness
talking to myself
and snow drifting through the window

I saw her face against the glass
where she found me
my shadow and my silence

waiting for her
for whom everything happened a first time

I remember how her hands undressed me
while I stood shivering beside the bed

I thought it had happened before

5.

she knows I am a left-eyed son
seeking an end to memory

she knows I am an animal of temptations
that I want to disappear
at the hem of her flesh

she will not read my cards
laughs and invites me to read her eyes
they are grey

I see my hesitation there
as each step crumbles beneath me
this is how life falls apart
on the porch as I reach to knock
and time and again step aside
just when light falls from the opening door

I recognize my pale defiance
I tell her it's all I have

this is what she says
that I can dream of anything
babylonian women
a black dog
anapurna

that   somewhere between yes and no
I can answer for myself

that I will end
how my kind ends
looking for other conversations
in other rooms

6.

stepping from shadow
I shivered beneath a streetlamp
there was never enough light

someone was singing
from a cellar across the street

. . . im dunkeln wird mir wohler sein . . .

I was waiting for lili
she would be wearing a yellow dress

or caroline otero
her lemon breasts
and spanish obscenities

words teased me into her arms
they were fine linen
sometimes silk or valenciennes
I felt them with my fingers
but they slid away
before I dould know I knew them
she took me into her lascivious bed

when I left I turned to the window
her oval face and dark hair
her red chemise
she was waving me goodbye

I raised my hand
but the sun shifted
and she was gone

7.

it's old-fashioned
being brave

ritter

always riding to another tournament

the usual true blue betrayals
meanness and small talk
but always   in the end   a need for honour

what else can a man do?
to find the woman
some days I catch a glimpse of her in my mirror

I follow

a stony river bed
an overgrown road

always riding past the tournament
into the desolate countryside

narr

8.

a pair of high heels
beside the stardust door

long beckoning fingers
saturn's wedding ring
and the overt stage

she lost her veils
asters blooming in the saxophone

I can't say it wasn't her
there was something familiar in the legs
they could leap mountains
but I had never before seen
the hunger in her eyes
and the fantasy in mine

9.

as if she knew I was standing outside the door
imagining her thighs or her slender back
she called me in   laughing
it wasn't the first time
she knew I loved to watch her undress

she was soaping her breasts
lifting
caressing
shaping them

she smelled of soap and spice
her hair was tied back

I'm bathing for you
now you must bathe for me

I removed my clothes
and stepped into the water
she reached up and drew me down

telling me about her day
she wrote in the water with her finger
as if I could read

I hadn't seen bare breasts all day
everyone out there wore clothes
I wanted to touch her beauty everywhere
and when she made a circle
with her index finger and thumb
I thrust my stick-up finger through

we had to laugh
the way our bodies came alive
and nothing much happening
how we knew our ways toward each other

we had to laugh
the way I wanted to relive life
like men before me   and sons
butting my way into the solar system

we had to laugh

10.

sometimes it begins with barking
a dog outside my window   or
the harsh bickering of jays

someone walking through my room
sets the globe quivering on its axis

niko knocks over a jar in the kitchen
I hear glass grind underfoot as he gets the broom

this is how I wake from my dream

this is when I begin to remember
the words I need

11.

she opens her lilac umbrella
and makes room for me

I can't help myself
it's the rain

somewhere it is midnight
and nothing in the mirror
a pillow slides to the floor

she hunches over him
one of them cries out   you can't tell who
they're lost in their helplessness

in the blind street outside
you can hear them mew and grunt
it's how you know where you are

but it drives you wild
wishing for love in a foreign city
long-legged women walking by
you imagine they're all passionate
in their rooms their clothes on the floor
kicking off their shoes
you imagine a room with six windows and maybe athenian light
you lie there in her bed
as she rides you past pleasure
until you can't take anymore
but you stay you want to stay
hinged like this

unhinged   somewhere
you are on the street
naked beneath her umbrella

it's the rain
it's everywhere
and I can't help myself

12.

her grey eyes gaze sometimes from my wall
or from the music in my room

she sends me postcards from the himalayas
a moon bear   a red panda

I keep meaning to ask if she's seen yeti
but the question never comes up
I think she's been there
though she pretends she hasn't
and she didn't take the photographs

often she is hard
and I think she hates me
but she's just angry
or doesn't care

she lets me off the hook
so to speak
she disengages me
to my captivity

there must be a better way to say
I don't want to lay down the cards

I remember now she was there
standing in front of a red stone house
she was wearing a silk top hat

one day I'll be there
on a treeless mountainside
giving up giving up

giving up

13.

there is something ahead
what I'm walking toward

around a corner
in a doorway

wherever my birthday waits

a pair of shoes

if she is there
they will fit

if it is the death of me

14.

oil spreads on the newspaper
my cat licks delicately at a last oyster

this week is nativity
next week the century continues on its grievous way

I am remembering the river

I am remembering
how the blouse slipped
from her shoulders

there is no other comfort

a dream of winter in her eyes
she puts her finger to my lips

a top hat at her feet

dream of the black river

I'm dreaming a dream of the black river where I can't swim I'm
    dreaming my last breath I'm dreaming how things are
    almost over I'm dreaming a possible swimmer with
    powerful arms to hold me
the river is cruel and cold I would drown for warmth
my legs dangle beneath me in the water my hands perform
    circles my lips are open for a kiss who will kiss them?

a figure on shore I can make it out someone knows I'm out
    here someone appears poised on a rock a diver about to
    thread evening air and enter this dark water
but no one moves there is only a pose of intention and nothing
    happens ever again

my darling lord take me all the way my fishtailing body my
    hearing my faithful tongue
show me early morning first light across yellow fields could
    crack my heart
I had eyes enough to see it all blue eyes that didn't care except
    to see and see and see
I stood in the long grass and turned around and around it was
    all there all the love its earth and flight and the rain at night
move me again my darling I used to unlace my shoes and go
    barefoot I walked through grass felt the earthworm's
    trembling tunnel sometimes I was so light I walked above
    ground it made me laugh my legs streaming with power or
    light I could see it shining in my veins I was a snake
    sloughing his life with no hope for another there was
    nothing to want or need or do there was nothing

nothing feels like something when you straddle a bough high
    in the sugar tree or ma's singing in the kitchen
when you love someone feels so light you could walk without
    shoes anywhere you could doff your hat and fly

my love take me away all the way to where my lies are true
take me beneath your umbrella of water that will be good
        enough for me to stand in the rain dreaming the dreams of
        the dead and living dogs barking in backyards
        remembering the love and terror that brought me here
my beauty lay me down and take me all the way I'm dreaming
        the dream of my death or someone is it doesn't feel like me
        anymore
he's gasping the river is in his ears he's banging at the window
        he wants to break into the swimmer's dream he wants
        another another

flicker and hawk

there are clocks that stand still there are doors that don't open
the summer has almost died and I won't grieve my angel's
    talking to me
I look up I look down I know where I am it's time to love again

love and anger inhabit all our rooms we should have torn apart
    years ago
what is this tenacity that makes us cruel and brings us together?
all argument and logic all sense tells us it shouldn't be
but here we are eyes meeting and I think I see you it's been
    months your eyes are harder now but something in them
    makes me shiver tonight something from that first
    recognition when you knew and wanted me
there's nothing I can do wariness falls away I would risk
    anything for that look it's what brought me here in the first
    place a tenderness
the door to my heart opens it swings open so easily I wouldn't
    have thought it possible
you step in you're a girl in a blue pleated skirt and white
    ribbons in your black hair I know your face you step in
    fearlessly and look about at the red and blue walls at bare
    furniture you sit cross-legged in mid-heart light from the
    open door falling on you I hear you laughing you're happy
    you're throwing kisses everywhere
is this why I'm here to give you room all the windows and the
    floor?
your kisses are free and burning I'm spread all over the room
    the sky woman everything rises or crashes around me and
    I'm willing to ride it out

lord history falls in the cracks that's a way of saying I don't
    believe a thing I haven't lived and known that I don't want
    to put my shoes on and I don't want to fly away
my hands are open my heart this is how I was born how I am
    when my man and boy stand
lord this love is strong even when it's on the edge when we find
    others to make us whole we're not everything to each other
    we're everything else and that's the juice you can't get every
    day

my sweet heart didn't we know all this time we stand apart we
    turn toward each other in our eyes all the love we know
    reaching for the adversary we see?
we are two people man and woman we are two cultures and
    two birds in different flights we are two elements
we have learned the odds and embrace them
we come together fire and water flicker and hawk this is what
    we know of love

an audience with the dalai lama
or, the old-fashioned pas de deux

on the one hand a leaf in the shrub beside you
on the other family and work
I have never seen God I have been empty and filled and empty
    again

what can I say about what I know?
hymns that come easily to my lips while I walk
an ancient anger and the bags I carry filled with hats and shoes

I don't think I know much beyond what I know
my left my right hand a leaf wife and children
and sometimes a stony eye

my room you wouldn't believe the books and clothes all over
    the floor the records and stamps the lamp my smell and the
    typer
nothing much has happened there if you think of it and I have
on the other hand nothing more has happened outside the
    room
I grew up with lilacs there are lilacs outside my window there's
    not much I can make of that
it's like looking at old photographs in a way like catching a
    second wind or an animal in me sniffing out its old grounds

sometimes I think I have a question I want to have a question
    about things that matter
my body used to give me pleasure still does but it's beginning
    to break down maybe there's a question here
my knees my eyes sometimes there's a ringing in my ears and
    who knows what's happening just now in my most hidden
    cell a small detonation
but it seems clear where everything's going
I feel a lot more stupid than I did is this wisdom?

listen my love is someone other than me this must be what I need
she goes on journeys you should see her walk toward the
    clearing trees making way you should see her in her
    wedding dress the hem wet in the grass
you should see her when she drops the armour of her veils

when she's away and it's late when I crawl into bed I find she's
    dressed the emptiness beside me with her gown
all night I'm restless I wake when my hand finds silk my legs
    want to wrap around her
no bed has ever been this empty or so full it feels like god

a man can't say what he is that he needs to rut like a plow knows
    earth that he loves it
that he bends his knee to words he loves this too falls insensible
    sometimes before the beauty of memory and ruin
sir richard manuel died a lousy death hanging there cold as a fish
I can't explain it just listen to any of his songs just listen to how
    pure and sad a man's voice can be when he wants paradise
    but his arms aren't long enough
some voices belong to everyone

the boy in me doesn't like conversations he's busy wants to be
    free a word for what he remembers he could have said
    captured surrounded or surprised
he dreams time before love when he could sing the words
    didn't matter only the voice he was
but the man in me accommodates love and loss contemplates
    smoke and mirrors from a distance
he moves toward religion like prey to the lion a leaf to earth or
    a fish to the hook

does the prey feel ecstasy as it kneels into the lion's need? its
    stem hardening does the leaf desire release?
no I don't look for answers the questions are old and will grow
    older I want something other than rhetoric or ritual maybe
    a gesture
my devotion to the lord is imperfect there's some fight left in
    me I may be hooked I am not landed

what's there is my room my hands on the typer my eyes we
    used to say what's the diff
my children chewing at my knees my wife smiling through the
    window where's she going or is she coming home? she
    loves me she loves me not she loves me
what's there is the usual concoction hubble bubble eye of newt
    babbling tongue the old-fashioned pas de deux me and you

sometimes mother's on the phone do I love her yes I do and I
    still have father's hat
no I haven't seen God I live with angels some fallen
I sing *have thine own way lord* half the time I don't mean it
my wife sloughs her gown my pants at my knees like some clown
my son with his other world eyes you could never know them
    or their danger
or my daughter's prayers at night when everyone's asleep this is
    a way she speaks
and this is what I know what I need to know I want to redeem
    love before it does me in

private ceremonies

I have asked friends to perform private ceremonies in europe
one tossed a good luck stone into the aegean
another prayed for me in a white church near athens
later she sent a postcard from a pub in gdansk
someone walked to the harbour in barcelona and made a wish
this is how I travel europe with spells and invocation
I visit europe hidden in my friends' hair
or leaping from their passports at borders

I haven't been to europe my tracks cover another world it's
    taking me forever to cross a blue town beneath an electrical
    storm the highway's shoulders where I stuck my thumb out
    for freedom and this tenacious city
there are streets that have been paths where I grew up the
    street of sugar trees and caragana bushes the street that ran
    past the funeral home you could see a corpse lying in its
    coffin beneath dim light late at night and the street leading
    out of town
in this city streets where bookshops stand a small bar streets
    with chinese restaurants or an italian club streets without
    reproach streets where I carried my daughter on my back
    streets where I dreamed other lives

today my footprints are in this home where I've walked every
    floor the walls and ceilings where I've lain in bed sick in
    body or mind where I've tended fevers and imbalances
    where I've walked to the door for the mail or to test my
    memory with God's obnoxious people where I've talked
    and listened many ways with my love where I've carried
    my children to bed at night singing or telling where I've
    stalked around the typer or slithered like a snake where
    I've blundered late into bed or bellowed or wept in rage or
    pain or sorrow or tiptoed in and out of closets and
    conversations where I've crawled or swept toward sex
    where I've danced away fears or just for joy
I've brought my body and words here and my strength I've
    earned money this is where my music plays this is where
    I've broken and mended where I've learned several sides to
    love

friends there are wars here and there is unbearable delight each
    betrayal meets a loyalty who knows where it ends
I can't contain it all sometimes I'm beside myself often death's
    right there
my love and I talk late there are many other things we could be
    doing there are other lives for us to live but we've chosen
    each other there is an allegiance we take the time to talk
    and touch and we take the time to forgive
I'm here where I live and wrestle where I'm father for my
    children and everything I can be for love

blue wind

albert street windows are mirrors this afternoon
a woman stops to see herself but the sun dips behind a cloud
        and she sees me instead
she's startled but doesn't turn she studies the possibilities of
        my face
it feels as if we're both watching a film maybe with oscar
        werner and simone signoret in it
I remember her eyes they're the blue eternity is when you're a child
the blue I dreamed in 1959 as the dalai lama crossed the himalayas
the blue piano in my home church on good friday morning and
        mother's soprano singing me toward resurrection

I'm not sure what's going on here whether it's remembering or
        words but something's running away with me and I don't mind
the woman's gone she may be blocks away thinking how our
        eyes met thinking that maybe we were in one of those
        european films where people meet through restaurant
        windows and make melancholy love all afternoon
maybe she's trying to remember where we've met before

I'm lost in the world yearning for black-haired women
        shaggy-haired black-haired women one who can heal with
        her hands another a lover in a red coat one who knows the
        day I will die and the one I just saw
explain it to me the woman who walked by her recognition her
        complete need for me and her indifference
explain this my sudden lust my laughter as the thin red doors of
        my heart rasp open and the blue wind blows through at last

listen to this stammering this voice as it caterwauls through its
        wounds and desire the barbed wire behind the eyes
listen to the heart today it's happy
this woman I know by the grace of mirrors I've seen her
an appearance in my life and my life bending like light as it
        passes earth

from

You Don't Get to Be a Saint

anna (first dance)

we walk from streetlight to streetlight
silence to silence
how to speak about the human heart and memory
how to speak about all the rooms we live in

anna akhmatova wrote love poems before the russian
revolution. everything changed. her former husband,
gumilyev, also a poet, was executed for unspecified reasons in
the early '20s. later, their young son was thrown into prison.
primarily, it appears, to keep akhmatova silent.

during the '30s a few poems were put on paper, a few of those
hand-copied and passed around. mostly akhmatova was
silent. in her heart and mind she wrote poems but, for her
child, she kept a public silence. these were the years of famine
and purges and show trials. akhmatova, along with friends like
the mandelstams and pasternak, never knew when stalin
would point at her.

after stalin's death, her poems began to appear in
publications. strangers often stopped her on the street to
thank her for the poems, not only for those few published but
for the unwritten ones they knew she had lived. if it's possible
for one woman's silence to save the soul of a nation, perhaps a
world, this is what akhmatova did. she lived her people's
silence, and their poems.

in the later '40s the commissar of culture, let him remain
nameless, publicly denounced and ridiculed akhmatova as
the "nun and whore" of russian literature. this referred to the
fact that akhmatova wrote love poems of several kinds, that she
lived and wrote equally in the spirit and the flesh.

akhmatova's silence of the '30s overlaps another kind of silence of the same time. alberto giacometti, who died in '66, the same year as akhmatova, was a swiss sculptor working in paris. for almost a decade he produced next to nothing. each sculpture disappeared. a few small figurines, small enough to fit into matchboxes, survived. giacometti kept sculpting, working toward what he saw, hammering, carving, chipping until there was nothing.

this was a silence. a silence of his materials, if not his process. through the rigours of this merciless vision his famous later sculptures emerged, elongated and thin, almost air. his work was not about objects. they almost disappeared. it was not about society. his work was about itself. his silence was about the act of seeing.

and akhmatova's silences were about being.

how to speak once more about the flesh and the spirit
the red heart and the blue wind

let's say it was 1958 *sail along silvery moon* was on the radio
it was sunday afternoon in july I remember the river and
        swallows swooping low over the water
silver medallions fluttering on their chests the catholic boys ran
        along the springboard and jack-knifed into the seine river
there was something ominous about the muddy water like a
        dream anything could be there venomous snakes weeds
        and roots to clutch at you or simply depth something
        ominous and those lean white bodies of faith disappearing
        with graceful dives

I held my breath each time wondering if this one would
    drown forever and not return how could he possibly rise
    from that darkness of river and overhanging trees how
    could the water give him back to light?
but always each boy exploded into air returning from death
    or dreams flinging wet hair from his eyes shouting defiance
    at the shore and each of us shivering there
and then the sun was so bright dancing in the spray around
    the diver's head so bright on his long arms cleaving water
    you could hardly believe in anything

let's say it was 1958 I was sitting on the fender of father's blue
    dodge and it was sunday and I didn't want to ever leave the
    river again

I was eating a persimmon trying to think of God it didn't
    work my tongue wouldn't let me get away with it
there are no miracles only mirages in the desert and
    disappearances in the river
there's nothing human that isn't betrayed and I know nothing
    but what's human my hands my tongue and my face in a
    mirror

grandmother wouldn't show me her photographs said I'd
    never know what I couldn't would I? her life before me
but I think I remember her in the orchard she was a girl her
    hair was soft and flowing down her back her legs brown
    with sun

she said sometimes there were angels in the orchard she saw
    them among the trees but she wasn't sure and if there were
    what should she do?
sometimes there was a black dog or the neighbour's boy with
    a stick sometimes there was nothing she could remember
    and she was running for her life
this is how she learned to pray she said this is how she
    worked her way out her hands at the clothesline her eyes
    on the sky

I don't love the prayer rug obedience or disobedience nothing
    that absolute I love the babylonian body and the human
    wound I love the surprising word the sinuous approach I
    like the world approximately
the way grandfather smoked a cigarette in the garden his feet
    lost among the potato plants the way he smiled and I
    smelled the drifting smoke his stories hovering among the
    raspberry canes the way he leaned on his hoe forever
I love words in the air balanced between mouths and ears I
    love the way they're smoke before they're stone
but it's true I think there's not much a voice can say there's a
    limit I guess to art there's no end to desire

stepping from shadow I shiver beneath a streetlamp there's
    never enough light
I'm waiting for her she'll be wearing black I imagine her
    undressing slowly my eyes are raw with looking

I imagine the beauty I see there are such possibilities in these
    distances
I almost jump from my skin I want to reach out to what I
    imagine

always knocking at the window maybe I'll find myself there
    each window a possible mirror
is this eros? longing for consummation in another place on
    another day?

I want to break the glass
I want to touch her everywhere

she knows I'm a left-eyed son
seeking an end to memory

she knows I'm an animal of temptations
that I speak out of desire
that I want to disappear at the hem of her flesh

she invites me to read her eyes
I see my hesitation there
on the porch as I reach to knock
and time and again step aside
just when light falls from the opening door

I recognize my pale defiance
I tell her it's all I have
that I don't want a way out
I want to walk in light
I don't want to be caught

she says that somewhere between yes and no
I can answer for myself

that I will end
how my kind ends
looking for other conversations
in other rooms

gregory told a story gregory's from kiev. there was a big fire, a fire so hot no one ventured within a hundred yards of it. barricades were thrown up and firemen tried to get enough pressure in their hoses to reach the distant flames.

the fire was raging out of control everything seemed lost until suddenly a firetruck sped down the street, smashed through the barriers and drove right into the heart of the burning building. a lone fireman leaped from the truck, grabbed a hose and flailed it in all directions. after ten or fifteen minutes the flames died down enough for the other firemen to move in closer and direct their nozzles onto the fire. it wasn't long before the fire was extinguished.

some weeks later a ceremony was held honouring the lone fireman who had courageously doused the inferno. the fire chief, and other dignitaries, praised him fulsomely, and they awarded him $5000. when he handed over the cheque, the chief asked what he would do with the money.

"well," he replied, "the first thing I will do is repair my brakes."

I love her hands the way they touch the garden
I love her hands in water the way they move there or when
        she is silent how they heal
I love how she gathers the world with her hands and lets it
        slip

something about all the rooms I have inhabited the way they
    held and released me
rooms that were cloisters or rooms with lamps and seashells
    and empty bottles
rooms with pianos or angels rooms where voices died rooms
    that were dance-halls for wallflowers

something about rooms the way a room could be a heart filled
    with yearning the way the telephone suddenly rang and the
    room opened to the world

I remember the night my daughter was born a storm broke all
    the windows in the house when I returned home the wind
    was blowing through the rooms

rooms of prayer or despair rooms of light

I was standing at the window someone was knocking I went
    to the door but no one was there just children laughing
    down the street

I was caught in the rain it was the day I knew my death not
    everyone's that lucky
everything came together everything was there my footsteps
    behind my footsteps ahead my unborn children everything
    was there and I knew the number of my days but I lost it
my bones are white it's what I know from grandfather's farm
    what's left in the fall scattered bones where horses wheeled
    all summer the wind low in the grass and the sudden cold
    sweeping rain
I lost everything I thought I was and had didn't have a thing
    it was a lie I made didn't know I was that kind of god
    didn't know I'd believe my own memory

sometimes it feels like I'm sculpted don't know anymore
    who's sculptor who's shaped
like giacometti's figurines not carved from but toward
    something I'm sculpted into dust until there's nothing there
    or something like nothing
I must think this is some version of divinity what else to call it
    there's no purpose here there's nothing to know there's just
    this seeing this continual seeing
I must think this is leading somewhere that I am at that
    random moment when the chisel can't stop and chips a last
    feature into crumbs when I'm plaster dust in the sculptor's
    hair or his white footprints on the street

something about the river I heard ice grind in my sleep
something about rivers how they touch what we forget
there's no end to the river where we walk there's no end to
    our walk

it doesn't take much a scent of lilacs or rose oil a song it doesn't
    take much to remember the world always how it was the
    way memory spills through what I see or touch or hear and
    there's no end to it like desire

I remember there was no need for the altar icons or text I didn't
    know I was being tried
I was barefoot for a moment like grandmother before me
    looking for my shoes something to make me human I was
    looking for a hat not just any hat my hat I was looking for a
    hat

memory is a scar I love to touch but will never trust
the future because I was born I trust and can never touch
so I straddle time taking the scraps memory offers and
    wanting them again and again

grandmother at the clothes-line the sculptor's baffled hands
    grandfather leaning on his hoe
this is what I know until the end of memory

I walk with her she holds her umbrella above us like a petal
    like ribs holding a heart like the opening cage of the sky
we throw stones into the river we jump pools of water the
    moon's beneath our feet

I was eating a persimmon there's not much to believe or say
    there are mirages in the mirror yes I betray my tongue with
    silence I'm shivering with delight

–what a coincidence.
–what?
–a coincidence. that we met.
–oh.
–reminds me. I heard of a man, somewhere, walking down a
street. a baby crawled out a window, fourteenth floor, and fell
on the man's head. both survived. a year later, to the day, same
man walking down another street. a child leaned against a
screen window, fourteenth floor, screen gave way and the child
fell on the man's head.
–same man?
–yes.
–same child?
–uh huh. they had moved to a different apartment.
–they lived?
–yes.
–and then?
–and then? that's not enough for you?
–there's always more.

—well, there is. you can imagine the man had problems. his neck was never the same. it wouldn't heal. he visited a chiropractor. thought the receptionist looked familiar.
—it was the child's mother.
—no, no. listen. she looked familiar. he thought he must know her. he approached her and began a conversation. before long they realized they were twins. they had been separated at birth and adopted out. in different cities. let's say their names were bob and linda. well, linda had married a bob and bob had married a linda. they each had two daughters with the same names.
—what about the child?
—the child?
—the one who kept falling on the guy's head.
—oh. well, many years later, the child was a teenager, and the man, bob, was desperately ill and his sister had just died.
—same disease?
—of course. they had both divorced, moved in together, their kids were gone. just brother and sister sharing an apartment, helping each other along. well, she died and he was going fast, so he jumped from a tall building.
—same building where the child fell on him?
—I don't know. he jumped. hit a car stopped at a red light. flew in through the windshield, killed the passenger.
—wait. it was the kid.
—no. the kid was driving. it was the kid's mother.
—you're kidding.
—no.
—could make a person look up now and then.
—that's true. you never know what's going to happen.
—truth is stranger than fiction.
—or life.
—I guess.

–and here we are.
–a coincidence.
–I'm not so sure.
–listen.
–are you adopted by any chance?
–no. listen.
–I knew someone once looked just like you.
–I imagine everyone's got someone looks like them.
–your name. you must have a name.
–I'd rather not.
–let me guess.
–I won't tell you.
–well, then, I'll guess what your name isn't.
–listen, I've got to go.
–george.
–I'm not saying.
–lenny.
–listen.
–albert.
–I'm going.
–emile. frankie. vincent.

blue shoes

in the hottest summer alive with the sky appallingly blue and
    blind guilt burned out like a house on stilts
in the collapsed porch in everything that can't be retrieved or
    forgotten in the peeled paint on the wall
in the memory of the spear flying through childhood in
    hallowe'en masks in blue shoes walking relentlessly toward
    an end

when you're wide open with need when you call for someone
    and you become a naked voice bare of nuance and finesse
    of memory when you can't help yourself and you call
when you're a drum waiting to be struck a stage ready to be
    danced when you're at the mercy of love
when you're terrified when you shiver because you've been
    flayed when you laugh or cry at the drop of a hat when it's
    your hat
when you feel your way toward the frost and desolation of
    windows and just the possibility of a window where you
    can rest without bags and shoes without everything you
    have to do and be
when you move toward freedom meeting its necessities with
    hands up when you hear wind on the roof and you're
    expecting rain when you loosen and billow like a sail

someone in the world turns toward you and you've been
found and you give up
someone unbuttons you and washes your body the heaviness
lifts and because she has consented to be your need and
you become hers you are two children talking late and
laughing as if this is really how things happen
someone holds you for a moment at the foot of the stairs she
offers her window and you believe nothing because
everything's true your fingers on her collar-bone and she
leans to touch the light in your feet

it's impossible though after brilliant days of waking after
tenderness and gestures of affection
it's impossible how love like imminent death shows us the
river or tree for a first time and like death shuts our eyes
again
it's impossible love's bafflement as it turns a corner how we
return to our ordinary rooms how memory is a slow
assassin
it's impossible how we pass time a pair of shoes at the door
it's impossible the commotion of another birth

a woman from jamaica

I don't think it's too much to ask that for a moment every
    wound heal and stutter toward silence
I don't think it's too much to ask for a hesitation of the
    highball thundering through our veins
let's say we can halt fear let's say this room is enough that all
    streets and rivers flow here that all gods drink at this bar

I know a woman from jamaica who tells annancy stories she's
    laughing like a mischievous child
I know a woman who could outleg the obeah man and she
    has who could walk water and she will
tonight's her final dream what each of us will dream the
    world loosening and shifting like catastrophe but it's only a
    single death

is the music loud enough can you hear it on your skin?
are the chairs and tables dancing is the dolphin diving in?

a woman is dying when she takes my hand I feel the chill of the
    cold mirror she has held
a woman is dreaming annihilation hands reaching and
    rapacious wicked hands that harass her they want to break
    the mirror she raises it high above them with her thin arms
    she knows what this is this encounter with the end she has
    never stood a longer night
when it's over she says when jehovah's come and the mirror
    whole she'll see what is left her long body in death she'll
    know she was here in this blue place of water and grass

is the dream loud enough can you feel it on your skin?

a dying woman has climbed out of the dark agitation of prayer
   and terror with the ghost in her hands
a woman is walking by the water she leaves her shadow and
   the willow a woman is rowing away
I don't think it's too much to ask that for a moment every
   wound heal and stutter into silence
let's say we can halt fear let's say the music's loud enough we
   can hear it on our skins and the chairs are dancing the
   dolphin's diving in

dream of the world

there is a dream I have of anna in the doorway this is almost a
    memory of july a handful of clouds drifting in a monet sky
    and anna's sudden silhouette
this is a moment when I know everything when school is out
    and I'm dreaming irish this is when the world ignites in my
    eyes

there's a story where I'm prowling in the kingdom looking for
    shade I was wild once in my head I was wild in my heart
someone slipped through the garden's green and hoe I was
    coughing in a bush a suicide of leaves I had the sky and
    hawk I got gladiators on the brain

there is a dream where I'm drunk beside the road or it's father
    one of us at the end of himself there are black trees in april
    and I can't see the wind anywhere
this is a memory of sun and a consolation of shadow this is a
    day of keening and love and the end of fathers

it's a memory me praying the way children play me looking
    east and west nothing there nowhere nothing is never
    something nothing is what you breathe when god's on fire
there is a dream of empty pockets where I can't find my
    hands there is a dream where anna steps smiling from the
    door and I fly into another dream of the world

first step into air

a man leans out a window looking up and down the street for
   a familiar shape someone who just passed someone he
   might remember
sometimes it's a voice through the door half a conversation he
   once had or a song from the sea
he turns suddenly because there's someone behind him he
   almost knows who but it's only something ordinary like
   leaves rustling at the wall

a man stands at the railing of a bridge he's father and son he
   wants the river he wants the sky a man stands between
beneath this bridge is where lovers preen and children play
   this is where we spread our blanket
a man follows his shadow through the end of the day he's
   yearning for a body his if he can find it hers if that's where
   it is

he remembers mother's arm curved around him and the
   absence on the other side he remembers every song she
   sang
he knows the ballads and lullabies that made him prince or
   drowned man he knows the hymns of heaven
a man recalls his birth dazzling light on the harbour his proud
   father baffled in the tavern there is an embrace he needs

a man can't reach as far as he wants and reaches too far he feels
   flayed sometimes all bones and height and nothing to
   touch
grief is the word for this or grieving but his fumbling with the
   doorknob and the empty room where love lived there are
   no words for that
what can't be said has something to do with a man's first step
   into air it has something to do with mourning

feels we're near tears shivering and short of breath it's cold
    near the window and the air is thin
a man sits on his empty suitcase in an empty house he's not
    leaving this is an exile's return
we forgot we had these tears pain blossoms like an opening
    fist the heart demands its reparation

he keeps turning because there's nothing ahead always the
    voice is from behind and someone's tugging at his coat
there's a nagging almost a word on his tongue as if he's already
    said it yet he's only about to speak
he leans into the rain to watch the faces pass he listens to the
    singer on the street a man no longer answers to his names

blue flame

sometimes silence is sultry a restless heat and a gaping for breath
  sometimes it's a drone at the window and crawling skin
there are days when light leaves the animal's eyes and leaving
  the door it drags its belly beneath the house
there are no lamps or rings no spells to say only the word that
  will not come
she knows words like breathing she knows the silence that
  takes breath away there are no choices to be made

this cage is hard as flesh a blue flame beneath the skin and
  paper's white waiting on the desk
day after day she rummages at the keys for just a little music
  but all she finds is fear
each day slips away with random gestures the washing of
  windows the broom's work the forgetfulness of eating
nothing happens and nothing changes but her darkness is
  always as near as the mirror
something sifts through her fingers sun dust or words
  something passes and nothing's left to lose

it's in the waiting buried in the stifled corners of waiting that
  something shifts for a moment the curtain sways a shadow
  lengthens on the wall
she feels it inside her body an unclenching a small pain
  something of her own a birthmark she feels the animal
  stretch and shake off its death once again
the fox at her door deep-chested pelicans at anchor these are
  words standing on the beach in her footprints this is an
  unearthing of words
but to speak them is impossible she knows this she works
  only with echo with mimicry this effort of words is an
  empty room with a thousand windows
this is all the only salvage of waiting imprecise words the
  song you hear when you tilt your head someone humming
  behind you

fox

when the sun is high in the still afternoon when you turn
    from your desk to stretch and gaze out the window she is
    there
the gift of a fox how she keeps a distance yet meets your eyes
    intimately from the edge of the clearing
a small fire a moment of light nothing is as awake alert to
    everything outside her need almost a cat in dogskin
she steps sometimes with the fearing grace of a deer other
    times she struts like a princess before a mirror
a fox is what it is to be alone outside your family what it is to
    be absolute for a moment
her leaving is a sudden absence she leaves like breath you
    don't question it you don't await its return
wherever she is there is permission she lopes through a play
    of the world we yearn toward
her absence is a perfect forgetting not amnesia but the serenity
    of an empty day

solo

do nothing she said there's nothing you can do but he's dead I
    said he lay splayed on the road his mother pacing the
    shoulder her face stretched across her skull he's dead
    there's nothing to do she said come with me I heard the
    town snoring and wind sifting through our skins

you are fatherless she said his dead watch on my wrist and
    light through leaves caging my eyes I want to dance I said
    like flying barefoot and light as silver I want to touch earth
    for a moment

when you speak she said you move from what you know yet
    god is a word you long to find the world pours out untold
    stories when you are silent when your hand rests without
    gesture you are godless and the world without end

if god is a dancer I understand light and levity the foot
    pivoting on earth and I understand the cold sometimes
    dark intrusions on spirit its capture or release how flight is
    managed and ecstasy

do nothing she said god comes and goes with his clubfoot
    looking for the perfect partner it's never you for more than
    a moment she said he leaves you solo take heart

you're free she laughed if you want it a sad angel a ghost of
    yourself a traitor I turned from the dead his mother paused
    to watch something nudging her memory she raised her
    pale hand and waved

you don't get to be a saint

like stars snow's falling all over town
headlights are passing on the walls
a god's walking barefoot through the drifts

the town drunk's leaning against a tree
he sees a dead hand in the snow
and reaches down to offer his own

you don't get to be a saint the dead man says
you get to warm your hands for a moment
you get to catch your breath and say one thing

I can make you a wizard he says
I can give you life forever
but I can't take the price off your head

I don't want to be a wizard says the drunk
I live with the price and I don't mind dying
I just want to sing a lullaby

he clears his throat and sings the dead man to sleep
then he turns into stillness
like none ever heard ever more still than snow

New Poems

raining all over the world

rain in sheets and cold these weeks
but the heart pummels on
rain deepens the window
the world's slant
a bird with red wings circling for a reed
or a thing from muck
that turns in its tracks again and again
never where it should be
always where it is

rain is how love hides
behind curtains and glass
lovers wanting to lie in each other's arms
wanting to know their skin again
but afraid they will disappear
and their love not be enough

rain is a way ancestors speak
one way to say all is forgiven on the other side
that nothing matters anymore
it is silent there
but no one's talking about this side
that we do everything over and over again
that we never get out of debt
and the family photos carry on

some days it's raining all over the world
those are good days bearable days
days of interior conversation
but in every life there's a change of weather
everyone's got an old dream that returns
we are going back my dears
we are going back to the serengeti
the iron jaw and the drought
each animal torn by the unjudging teeth
of each

love's wheel

I remember her voice
reaching for me in the night
don't go don't go
her hand drawing me back
into the hidden water

and I loved her
and spooned her into sleep
memorizing her breath
the moon in slats across the bed

listening to her dream
of a child's holiness lost
in an unholy land
and longing for home

that was enough for her
that I listen to her body all night
holding her
enough that I lie there
with her on love's wheel

somebody loved me

and somebody loved me
her smell all over my skin
remembering words from her mouth
words in time
a voice coming through the line
like something holy but not
and I'm wondering how it disappears
how I keep going through the funerals
and always something on the other side
something but never what was
still I've got it with me in the flesh
that perfect rememberer
my tongue my ears
her voice in the world
a lost moment
a whisper of love a sad blown kiss
caught by the wind

finding god

I can sing that's all not much of a commodity nothing to scrawl
   on my resume just something I've found again
finding god in a God-riddled world finding love her feet in my
   hands her tired body loosening into sleep
lying beside her past understanding curled against the world's
   map the curve of her shore

I can sing like a child gathering stones or an old man rounding
   the corner with his eyes full of night
finding god in my nightstand drawer a blue shell from a beach
   a bottle of danish glass and a dozen letters of love
in her sleep she turns into my arms and sighing back to dream
   she's sheltered for a moment in the world

I can sing to the cold stars and lake I can sing to the city where
   lovers' rooms gather dust
finding god in the absence of the come-on shrug of her
   shoulder the absence of her scent
falling through fear and sorrow through dreams of my
   companion in her shawl and tears

I can sing on a broken bridge with a broken child I can sing
   when there's nothing else to be done
finding god in the night rumble of a distant train finding god in
   the memory of my bruised skin
nothing's meant if it doesn't happen living a diary of finding
   god a small pretension of words

remembering emily again

light on the stairs
where angels have come and gone
light on the wall
revealing the faint handprints
of a leaning apparition long forgotten
the shape of a spinster
a woman dizzy with words
clinging to the bannister for a moment
then turning back to her long room
where the world is

shh (the window)

shh there's only one of me awake a rogue my darling the
mischief shh before doing before action lie low let the sleeping
dog lie chained to its obedience and love the open morning
window its breeze and sparrows and mountain ash a fly at the
screen love my son's footsteps creaking in the kitchen the
covers cool my feet sticking out love the rise and fall of my
chest air moving through my nostrils love memory the poplar
leaves shimmering in july in a far off town pretty girls madlyn
or joey with teasing eyes someone singing *rock me baby* on a car
radio on town line road shh he's stirring I feel him stirring
waking to the words come on and slide back to the window
here the rectangular sky opening up shhh

gathering bones

what happens after leather the doorway filled with rage what
    happens after thunder and stones after muscle and broken
    glass what happens after the brain explodes and the heart
    clenches on a memory a wraith in the basement a wrath
    what happens after the son after the trumpet?
a father leaning in the family rubble of walls and old words and
    swallowed songs the one-eyed man on his back among the
    roots the jack watching his boy dancing in the abbatoir
a father at the window with a putty knife his last stand against
    chaos a father with a shivering spine and a heart attack a
    man arm-wrestling with a spook
what happens is a man drowning in the maelstrom of his heart
    the banks collapsing and overrun and overgrown what
    happens is a helplessness a return to everything unnamed

a man gathering bones and bellowing in the marsh a place of
    reeds and mud a man seeking his consolation
a five-bone rider on his rocking-horse a child wrapped in
    mother's arms looking for a way out of the rhythm a
    barefoot child without a river
five-bone rider lusting for woman's hair and smell rampant in
    her bed he is five men insatiable in her womb ravenous to
    be born and greedy for death a lout sucking at her tit
a man riding a horse like words across the fields five-bone rider
    on his way from the ancient trees to the city
through dry riverbeds molluscs and small spines of fish the
    rider with a bone for each direction and one for the sky

galahad with his gauntlets and his grail the emptiness of a
      perfect medieval sky a holy man with grendel on a leash all
      the accoutrements and fashions of fear
what happens is the surgery of a battlefield legs with their
      boots on a hand with a twitching ring finger what happens
      is the lord's evisceration god in the saddle
a father with his virgin heart trying to pray his way past the
      bully in the mirror a father in his faces working to hold the
      world together
nothing happens power is an impatience a restless turning from
      the window nothing happens the doorway fills and empties

resurrection

I've kept myself in the basement
listening to the machine grinding to a stop
I've kept myself beneath the stairs
overhearing conversations among the demolition men

I've stood sideways behind cemetery trees
hearing the elegies and tears
I've wandered among the stones
listening to the wind blow

I've kept myself for love
each kiss the first
each caress an astonishment
hard not to be religious
when you're laughing so hard
or weeping
and I step off the back porch once more
with a drumming heart

I've kept myself for the disintegration of things
a shabby garden and the river
epileptic children on the streets
the well filled with stones

I've kept myself for the face shifting behind everything
behind a drunkard's leer
a prophet's words
and a bereft lover's eyes
behind the face the bartender offers to the world

I've kept myself for this
the house leaning east
windows broken
and doors swinging in an april wind

I've kept myself
for the resurrection
the child
jumping from my knee
to play

dreaming a fox

city's falling around my ears
birds banging against the window pane
all night I dreamed a fox crossing the snow

my memory of its golden fur
of its fleeting eyes
a memory that has been frozen by love

and I'm laughing inside
smiling at the fox
and the golden dream of snow

blasphemous wheel

a gust of wind at my window a distant thunder the smell of
    approaching rain
awake in the world's stillness I am a coastline of skin with
    bones rattling through the day and remembering everything

the nakedness of a bare-backed boy with arrows all sun skin
    and wind a thief with a stolen name
a child from trees his memory long and strong and dangerous
    to mothers and fathers

remembering a young man's beatitude his walk in that pale
    light of angels trusting the muscle of his heart
flinging my hat at the stars the euphoria fevers and scars of love
    a dying that makes the body beautiful

waking from the astrologer's dream kneeling there in my
    cassock reading his fingerprints all over the sky
everything written in stone jesus schadrach and judas the long
    arm of love on my shoulder and me rehearsing my
    disappearance

from the body the clutching body the whole wide family
    embrace disappearing from blessed love
from my body my desire disappearing from the touch a kiss a
    handshake the flesh surrendering

and disappearing I found my father on his way to heaven his
    body scrawled with worry and work
found the river where anna was born where she let everything
    go gathering berries in her apron

living there with a grappling hook and rope with a handful of
    words to curse and pray
a ranting mister in his shabby coat a man who licks stones
    remembering the alphabet

some friday nights anna visits me beneath the bridge to talk
    about the world and admire the stones I trade for words
she loves me with that old face claims me with her impish eyes
    I have one pocket to empty

children are executed in slums by policemen she says children
    on needles and fumes are looking to vanish
and the ancient stone people slaughtered in some clearing
    because they're still there they're still there

the world's stupidity from the first splitting everything in half
    and looking for paradise
and me with a lunar hook and innocence love spreading from
    heart to brain and back again

waiting for rain a caress something a touch in the world a wind
    a hand maybe the bird rising from a reed
warming my feet at the bonfire of crazed theology and
    revolution speaking finally of love and sorrow

don't always know who's tongue I am just speaking from
    memory all those things crawling out of the long night
lucy playing horseshoes in the great rift uncle josh at prayers
    and anna in her flowered hat smiling for the camera

can't help looking for the disease its rapture despair and delight
    its faithlessness
finding love on a lucky day someone singing on the beach and
    walking away

and I can't forget the song its dazzle and gospel I can't forget
    the singer in her loneliness
and I'm back in my flesh I can't leave nor do I want to leave
    this wicked world in its ordinary pain

who is it at the window leaves shivering at the first drops of
    rain the house opening to the storm
there's lightning in the basement as above so below they say I
    want to kiss the world as it sweeps by

saying yes to the blasphemous wheel lord god condor hovering
    like an umbrella saying yes to tongue and teeth to love's
    gentle breast
saying yes at the table an animal snarling at my feet their hands
    moving over bread saying grace saying grace

absence of angels

I'm learning the absence of angels and the friends I encounter
    move with care around my soul
I still know the world is real but it doesn't look or feel that way
    even my body is something apart and silent
it's an awkwardness living inside an invisible building long
    halls and wide rooms whose walls evade me
like an animal twisting through underbrush snuffling for a den
    a warm hollow beneath a fallen tree looking for a place of
    sleep
my head filled with the smell of smoke and the taste of metal
    on my tongue I wouldn't mind going drunk
words dance on the page I can't focus one ear hears music the
    other listens to some strange pre-historic conversation I
    remember neither
just moving through my days the shakes when I wake fear of
    the day avoiding my bed at night afraid I won't sleep
in between the ambiguously ordered daytime hours of jobs and
    duties and collapses into the warm forgetting water of the
    bath
at night after late work after endless distracted reading of books
    to put off the moment of sleep's failure after pills an
    unsweet and deeply embraced sleep of anonymity

grazing my palms with her fingers diane once said I had
  invented myself that one hand belonged to me the other to
  my people's history
my mother grieves at my retreat to lick my wounds she says I'm
  like my father in his solitude and I hardly knew him
some days my son is disgusted by my rituals of disintegration
  how I stare at the television how I walk up and down the
  stairs between clumps of words in the basement and a
  restless examination of the upstairs rooms
he knows I'm killing time with the tv maybe he knows that I'm
  looking for memory in the house
the man who invents himself keeps a quick eye on landmarks
  remembers each day each word like a roadmap
the blinds swaying at my birth mother says an electric storm
  rumbled in the distance lighting the window
sugar trees in 1951 the poplar at the corner of the lot the weeks
  of learning to throw a curve in 1956 massacre on the
  curaray
the fires of conversion and its rejection the leather in front of
  the furnace the sounds of words all those years
eyes and ears stories and fragments of sense and nonsense
  dreaming alone among the raspberry canes in july the
  red-winged blackbird's song
hopkins and tillich in 62 *sailing to byzantium* in 1966 the young
  woman in the river with seaweed on her naked thigh

if I could see these days as a journey myself a traveller I could
imagine a purpose a point of arrival
talking and writing myself into some story that lets me get out
that makes a mathematics of the mess
if I could part the waters jackknife my way into someone's
memory find the man I've misplaced someone may
remember him
all I know I have to drive the smoke from my brain the smell of
crops burning the countryside in flames
I need to shave clip my nostril hairs I need to put on a tie the
only tie I love the white and burgundy one from nancy
I have to get out of these soft slippers and try my blue shoes
there's a possible direction to something I know
clothes make me stand up to the mirror looking at something
not quite me a man dressed for busyness for a walk down
broadway
the armor of my penetration into some kind of reality and I
begin to smell it and the smell is acrid not the soft smoke
of my dream
and my tongue in its white shirt and suit stammers a bit like
the computer's hesitation when it's fully loaded
but tongue finds its gift has the world's memory and the teller
of history lowers its expectations to the hard chase of dead
words
and I'll take a drag that's another smoke this tongue wraps itself
around and I'm back looking for sleep and a general with
his crack division to slaughter my fear at bayonet point
and where the hell are the angels? is this something they do?
dancing on the head of a pin? disappearing when you need
them? letting you meet the awakening sword?

my movie

this isn't my movie is it? 3 a.m. panics and heart attacks
    unhealthy early morning phone calls
this morning an old lover offered me a ride to the cemetery and
    I asked *who's funeral* she said *yours*
I guess it's one way for love to have gone and I appreciate the
    thought a kind of wake-up call
tonight I've got the knock-out drops slumping through my
    veins strange how they wake me up
first van morrison then mckennitt on the player got a
    hankering for some jazz improvisation
high hat sizzling the saxophone alive and everyone's brain shuts
    down for a well-deserved rest
only fingers and arms and lips the way the body all of it knows
    music like god knows earth
sounds like something safarik said amongst all the speed and
    range of his amazing mind

can't be my movie I've seen it before in some dive of a theatre
    playing two for the price of one
and the knock-out drops slow down the all-night races in my
    head waking me like amnesia
and there's nothing in the way for a midnight dive off the high
    board into the dark where the water's got to be
not a splash clean dive slicing like a scalpel through grey matter
    grey water into lost memory
strange way to live and die useless forays like some distracted
    archaeologist of love
what comforts me in the night is the sound of my son banging
    into the wall as he rolls over in his sleep
and I crawl up the steps to listen at his door to his cough the
    rustle of sheets and some faint music from a dream
you can see the musician in him his hands the release of his
    body at the drums you can see the distance in his eyes

this fall is older than any fall I've ever lived and the inevitable
bloody winter right on its ass
spent the evening with a friend a beautiful woman who has to
laugh at the stupidity of lovers
I agree with her but it doesn't stop me remembering how our
bodies met but didn't really get to know each other
and I'm thinking we're both feeling we ought to take a second
chance but it could be nostalgia
so we hugged I stammered something about her beauty and me
she said laughing I wasn't bad for 47
somehow listening to this celtic music these nights sounds like
wind and sorrow something forlorn
thinking how far I've gone from my people thinking of roads
and angels thinking of the tired heart
and the blessing of music driving me through the night the
song carrying me home and the voice always the voice

looking for a tattoo

listening to sandy denny I'm remembering copenhagen in
     february per and I wandering along nyhavn looking for a
     tattoo
per thinks a white tiger maybe but I don't have any ideas really
     a name a heart something to call me sailor
I watch tina in the blonde mirror cutting my hair in some shop
     on bredgade
she's beautiful but she's complaining no one asks her out men
     are so intimidated by beauty
walking toward the petersborg cafe with nina she's wondering
     what the word *spiritual* means not trusting it at all
she's got the legs of a girl playing on a beach and the old
     woman watching from behind her eyes
niels in the cafe smoking his yellow pipe and I'm thinking van
     gogh at the french mines except niels isn't wired like that
he's got the long memory of a father's hands at work and prayer
     a sexton's spade and a pair of boots

she's singing *listen, listen* a song that reminds me of home some
     true place I've been
thinking of the baltic I stood there in slow snow melting on my
     face almost feeling I belonged
thinking of my town its angels and ferocity remembering the
     bodies of people on their way somewhere
abandoned christmas tree in the alley a few strands of tinsel
     glinting in the cold light of a quiet new year's day
thinking of love's decisions each caught in each tenderness and
     the terrain of betrayal the animal heart in its den
nothing's home like love and it's not often anyone's home for
     long but it's something isn't it for a moment
the boy I been yes sir mister I can't put my finger on it but I
     was town world and heaven
letting go any morning or afternoon nothing much happening
     and everything going on

134

in my room sitting at the window gulls circling my head and
      grey light washing down classensgade
I've got the phone in my hand ready to call home but it feels
      dead and I've run out of words anyway
I've been in love and there's not much to say except nothing's
      the same though it looks that way
and it's still there what you've had doesn't go away love's still
      there like drifting smoke
you've got to be grateful for the grace of memory the way it
      makes sense of what matters
I've never been much for gardening back yard's gone wild my
      shoes need polishing and I've got to shave
so many ways to keep yourself civilized and walking the wheel
      sometimes you have to let go
it's copenhagen I like it I don't want to go anywhere anymore I
      think I'll get a tattoo and sail

room 502

bring me back copenhagen wind at the window there is no
    map for this place no violence of discovery or name
candles keep death and nothing at bay the fragility of breakfast
    the gratitude and grinning desire at daybreak
bring me back gulls and bicycles yellow tulips lighting a room
    at dawn the sleepless man slipping through his
    unbelievable dream
the prince at the wall this is europe poets at their books *yes and*
    no their world's reeling down the pages
bring me back to this fishing village sloping to the baltic a soft
    maze of snow melting into the roofs and the sea

talking new york: waiting on love

seems though that words are dead and me standing here with
    empty pockets and a mouthful of stone
you'd think I'd be humbled by this but I have no inclination for
    the desert and humility's hard work
you never get used to the waiting not me waiting on love
    waiting on the words you serve
hell I'm not used to being on this planet never mind the
    ballroom or the intricacies of table talk
I'm still feeling my way around all tongue and hands and ears
    each cell looking for a way in or out
I'm still dealing with disbelief not in anything particular but a
    kind of daily incredulity
for me everything's still pretty incredible I mean I get mystified
    by the same things again and again
like there's something missing and search and destroy never
    finds it though it's got a cemeteryful of cadavers
and you can read the tombstones with your hands and you've
    learned nothing but you love the feel of the letters
and I figure there's nothing missing I just can't put a name to it
    and that's all to the good
it's something in the feel of those letters the feel of granite flat
    and angular as it slips grainy into an A
there's something there the skin and imagination working
    together for the sake of working together
and it's there in the breath that you bring to the keyboard the
    breath that works its way into the words
you can feel them shuffle or shimmy or hoof it the way they
    take off as the breath shines its way
and you don't have much to say it kind of caught on once you
    abandoned yourself to the rhythm
I don't have anything to say outside what I know and that
    keeps shifting with the years
what I mean is not always what I say we all know that but
    you've got to sing it or hum it you never know

and when it sounds just right the words don't harden as fast
    they drift like stray notes always getting away in time
and isn't that the way to be caught talking like this while I'm
    waiting for word from my love

talking 3 a.m.

charles and irene are in love and the rest of us are fluttering
    through their light
they kiss and mew and can't touch each other enough they
    hardly need food their eyes are each other's menus
margie says she can tell per is in love too but his love is at
    home across the table casey ducks the question behind
    cautious eyes
what else to eat in these circumstances but raw fish what else to
    do but pay the bill and head for the dante?
winding through movie streets in the rain we lose charles and
    irene to the necessities of love
down bleeker street toward mcdougall with some folk song
    from the 60s running a silent track through my head
everything's a movie in this city has been or will be and that
    seems right my own life's a film that's rewinding

jazz is playing at the edges of everything like flames like
    splintered hymns behind god's back
it's playing in my head like crazy obituaries like revelations like
    nothing I can possibly say
nijinsky tearing at his eyes and hands the savagery of some
    music its relentless ransack
margie's talking from someplace outside herself I love to watch
    her step through the veils
the smoke is too much and I go outside where the rain has
    stopped I'm looking for something to know
and wouldn't it be a hoot if this wasn't hallowe'en and those
    were really ghosts in the streets?
and wouldn't it be something let's say to run into my father
    looking for work or anna playing tricks with the traffic?
but tonight I'd rather be walking down bleeker street in love
    and loved you know what I mean arm in arm the orphan
    in his dream

inside the dante per is the beatific man and he is though I
    haven't asked his family if they agree
I think I'd better stay near him you never know what rubs off
    and I haven't got heavenly ways
so what ways have I? what is it I am this time around? what's
    the lowdown on this machine?
I is what I am or some other zen popeye piece of shit you can
    pick up at any fast food joint or the desert
what I understand now that I am not a lover and never have
    been not the seething kind
I have not been conquest or conqueror god and goddess
    pursuing each other I have not been curly-haired and
    dangerous
I am what I am father to many I didn't ask for that I have no
    destiny I used it up in the wars
now I work for others I could be a waiter in the caffe dante
    with an apron and a shit-eating grin
I could work alongside the blonde norwegian waitress we all
    fell in love with on hallowe'en night

no I am not curly-haired and I serve many my face does not
    give away the seraphic lout
I am blasphemous in my desire I worship on my knees my
    tongue slippery on her pearl a current stiffening her limbs I
    find what I am not
you could say I take my religion seriously it makes me laugh
    the unbelievable tease and drive of the holy fuck
I have grown old to find what my young body missed a
    mockingbird on the roof a serpent in the roots
I have grown old to find my innocence the child licking stones
    memorizing earth's first fire

what I want to say is something about love it's 3 a.m. here
    november 1 on lexington where chris died in august
something of him remains in this place a feeling of the grace of
    his leaving an effortless leap
margie's soft voice grieves this man this brother as she slowly
    turns from the window
it's 3 a.m. and I'll assume it's 3 a.m. in everyone's life and I want
    to know what's become of us
I want to know the heart how it beats its way toward death
    gathering the world inside it
it's 3 a.m. and there are no betrayals only the child's disbelief as
    he tumbles from god's lap

it's 3 a.m. and I remember the fall of pale silk from my love's
    shoulders the length of her arms her slender thighs
remembering again and again what matters losing the rest in
    small blowouts of the brain and the radio's noise
I want to say something about love how it's flesh only for a
    while how it's words for a long time
and I want to weep here in new york city on hallowe'en I want
    to weep for us dying for a touch
this is any city any movie this is the music we make at the caffe
    dante our ghosts hovering around us

it's 3 a.m. and I want to say something about love that I have
    loved those I fathered and they have loved me
I want to ask the world to look upon my son and daughter
    with some tenderness I ask angels to carry them in their
    wings

companion

I am there
in the caffe sophia
or walking
by its window
I am in your sleep
when you turn
half-awake
into the memory of me
I am the voice
whispering
when you turn a page
in your journal
this is not a haunting
I am that other part
of you
the companion
who will never leave
living quietly
in shadows
asking the most of you

beloved

reaching for a heart a love
in this life a caress
at the small of the back
a hand a wrist

how you stir
in your sleep toward
the curve and bone
of the beloved

in the morning
a silence the sun
across the room
a hair on the pillow

stepping out of old skins

flying into new york a monk without God at least some cheap
    priest with silent hands and no beads
the world is eternal when you know it's coming down fast and
    the undertaker's measuring you with his gaze
there's no quarrel with god this is two-bit stuff everyone
    screwing someone and talking to the end of the street
everything happens when no one's looking red roses in the
    alley you could say or paydirt

nightfall and rivers reaching into the canvas the obscenities and
    assaults of a dark joy
pollack crashing through the window called to the bar I'd say
    strong-arming his way through hell
you could hear his brain grating against the inside of his skull
    no words coming and the dynamite lit
what do you do when all the schools collapse you're fucked
    anyway and butchered across the city?

o'hara fingering the typer he had the greek in him and how can
    you tell where he is anyway with that smooth face?
and that stupid death in the sand such an absence of reality a
    beach film gone wrong
o'hara slipped by everyone day after day something narrow and
    pale something sad beneath the words
all that talk and beauty the divinity of the nights and o'hara in
    his undershirt leaning out the window

and this is the world here look down the street moments of
    light and too much action
a horse grazing on the sidewalk someone cut him loose his
    rider's long gone lost
time to jinx the mirrors and look it in the face the squalor of
    the bored soul
time to come clean babies gathering at the ruins or o'hara's
    grave time to come clean

illness is what it's about writing our way through our diseases
    prayer anger ecstasy despair
writing for eve those twilight hours that shiver into something
    parallel another color another man
I am those hours 3 a.m. hours at work at work that's it what I
    am poet stepping out of old skins
hear that rattling a beggar's cup working the blind street the old
    man shuffling on his bones

the heart shifts

your eyes she says
say it all
what I ask
let's not talk
about that word
she laughs

two wary hearts
knowing what
they can't say
for a while
baffled by miracle
and loss

old things fall
slowly away
we touch with
the deliberation
of those
with time

more than desire

there is one thing
beyond your body
something past
your hand
this yearning
that is more than desire
my love
in your absence

your slender back
beneath a summer dress
your mocking
green eyes
you are an earthly gift
in my arms
a yearning
that makes me man

these are simple things
a basin of water
a mirror
the bracelet on your wrist
simpler yet
when you're away
is the love
that's left

gorgeous coat

I'm not asking the world
a companion
someone to walk with
through fire
through pearly gates
someone who'll reach out
and touch my neck
someone
to see me out

it's the rapture
on osborne street
your eyes
the green windows
of sweden
the old woman
you've always been
the beauty
you are

it's midnight
in the winter
you're walking
beside me
in your gorgeous coat
and there's no one
anywhere
on this silent street
to heaven

Translations

from The Shunning   page 34
O that I had a thousand tongues (from a German hymn)

turning home   pages 57 and 58
2.
the blessed hours . . . . o glimpse of light

mother
still joy in your playing
with the chinese   with my children
your sly blue eyes   the supple legs
a young girl who doesn't belong anywhere
except to the child inside   the memory of trees

still reaching from shadows

god's child

3.
mother
with you
I am completely
without you

nothing in the mirror   pages 63 to 78

das grab ist leer	the grave is empty
vater sterbt	father dies
tod	dead
kalt	cold
wasser	water
. . . im dunkeln wird	I shall feel better in
mir wohler sein . . .	the dark
ritter	knight
narr	fool